Name ____________________________

Address __________________________

Blank Classic

Graph Paper Notebook
(*Science*)
97 numbered pages - 100 total pages
Large 8.5 x 11

Design © 2021 Blank Classic



*Blank Classic*

*Mailing address:*
Blank Classic
PO BOX 4608
Main Station Terminal
349 West Georgia Street
Vancouver, BC
Canada, V6B 4A1

Cover design by: Lauren Dick
Interior design by: Lauren Dick

ISBN: 978-1-77476-204-2

FIRST EDITION / FIRST PRINTING

1